Wilfrid Laurier

Martin Spigelman

Fitzhenry & Whiteside Limited

Contents

THE CANADIANS®
A Continuing Series

Wilfrid Laurier

Author: Martin Spigelman
Design: Kerry Designs
Cover Illustration: John Mardon
The CANADIANS® is a registered trademark of Fitzhenry & Whiteside Limited.

Fitzhenry & Whiteside acknowledge with thanks the support of the Government of Canada through its Book Publishing Industry Development Program.

Canadian Cataloguing in Publication Data

Spigelman, Martin, 1948-
Wilfrid Laurier
(The Canadians) Rev. ed.
Includes bibliographical references and index.
ISBN 1-55041-481-X

1. Laurier, Wilfrid, Sir, 1841-1919. 2. Prime ministers – Canada – Biography – Juvenile literature. 3. Canada – Politics and government – 1896-1911 – Juvenile literature. I. Title. II. Series

FC551.L3S65 1999   971.05'6'092   C99-932549-3
F1033.L37S65 1999

© 2000 Fitzhenry & Whiteside Limited
195 Allstate Parkway, Markham, Ontario L3R 4T8

Prologue

O n February 20, 1919, all of Canada paused to honour a great
leader who had died two days before. Canadians, so often
torn by differences, were for once united. They came
together to praise Sir Wilfrid Laurier, to acknowledge his
contribution to Canada's greatness, to express their respect and love
for this elegant man. In the Ottawa cathedral, two funeral orations
were delivered, one in French and one in English — a symbol of

The Laurier funeral procession in Ottawa

Laurier's enormous efforts to bring French and English Canadians together.

Leading Canadians from all walks of life gathered in the cathedral. Outside the building, they were divided by politics, social views, culture, language and religion. But inside, each joined in Bishop Mathieu's and Father Burke's lavish praise of Sir Wilfrid. Fifty thousand Canadians paid homage to Laurier while he lay in state. Parliament adjourned for a week as a mark of respect for the man who had served Canada so selflessly. Thousands spent hours lining Ottawa's chilly streets to view his funeral procession.

Wilfrid Laurier had spent a lifetime trying to unite Canada and give it a sense of purpose. That was an enormous task in a country sharply divided by language and culture, region and religion. Laurier confronted these divisions, overcame some of them and succeeded in giving Canadians the most prosperous years they had known. His 15 years as prime minister were successful ones marked by massive immigration, trade expansion and unparalleled economic growth. They were years in which Canada attempted to define a new status for itself within the empire and within the world at large.

Laurier, like every politician, welcomed economic and national growth, but his driving concern was always the reconciliation of French and English Canadians. He ardently strove to end their mutual distrust and antagonisms. Many politicians, less scrupulous than he, were willing to exploit these hostilities for their own political purposes. Laurier would not. Although he too was a zealous politician and although he loved the power of the prime minister's office, he would never consciously divide the country for his own political gain. His speeches and policies were designed to lessen prejudice and increase tolerance. Laurier was a conciliator who tried to appease all factions in order to bring them together to build a united Canada. His ultimate goal was Canadian unity and everything else gave way to that commitment.

After Laurier's death, St. Lin, his birthplace, requested that his remains be buried there. Arthabaskaville, site of his country home, made the same request, as did Quebec City, his political base for over 40 years. However, Laurier did not belong simply to any one of these places. He was not just a Québécois belonging to one province, or a lawyer concerned only with legal issues. He was first and foremost a Canadian and his chief concern was always with Canada and its problems. His loves were Canada, Canadian unity and the Liberal party. Symbolically, Laurier's remains were buried not in Quebec but in Ottawa, the capital of all Canada and the centre of his attention for so many years.

Chapter 1
In Training for Canada

Laurier earned respect across the country because he symbolized Canada itself. His roots, like those of many French Canadians, dated back to the early history of New France and the very beginnings of Montreal. The first of the Laurier family in Canada, Augustine Hébert, knelt for mass with Jeanne Mance and the Sieur de Maisonneuve in the 1640s. Members of Wilfrid Laurier's family had settled the land and explored a continent; his ancestors had lived through the English Conquest in 1759-60 and shivered nervously while English troops with their different language and religion marched into Quebec City.

As the English and the Anglo-Americans from the southern colonies assumed control of Quebec, French Canadians, including Laurier's family, retreated into rural parishes where they thought their culture would be secure. Laurier's ancestors gradually spread out from the Island of Montreal to the Island of Jesus to the dense woods of Lachenaye. Later they moved up the Achigan River and the eighth generation of Lauriers took up residence in St. Lin, only 40 kilometres up the Achigan from the landing place of Augustin Hébert.

St. Lin was a pleasant, typical rural town. Close to the Laurentians, surrounded by virgin forest and with two straight streets dominated by a stone church, the town depended upon the agriculture of the farmers around it and upon the timber extracted from the forest. Here Carolus Laurier, a government surveyor and a pleasant, independent man, settled and married. On November 20, 1841, his wife, Marcelle Martineau, gave birth to their first child, Henri Charles Wilfrid. Marcelle died seven years later, but in that short time she instilled in Wilfrid an appreciation for his own heritage and for culture in general.

Wilfrid Laurier was born into a troubled and tumultuous time which he and his generation would never forget. In 1837, Louis-Joseph Papineau, the respected, if somewhat unstable, nationalist leader of French Canada, lead his group of Patriotes in an uprising designed to end British misrule. Papineau stood for French-Canadian rights but was beaten by a vindictive English army.

Following the rebellion, a number of French Canadians were executed, others were banished, while still others languished in dark, damp cells. Papineau himself had been forced to flee his beloved homeland for a decade of exile in the United States and France. Lord Durham's famous Report followed the rebellion and this in turn was followed by the forced union of Upper and Lower Canada. The new united Assembly, bringing together 550,000 English with 450,000 Canadiens, was designed to punish and assimilate the French Canadians. Few of them welcomed this arrangement, but they were powerless to resist its imposition.

The stories of this period affected the young Laurier. He learned that British rule was not always benevolent and that English Canadians were not always tolerant. However, he also learned that only defeat and despair would come from direct military or political confrontation. Challenge only hardened English resolve and encouraged them to use their formidable powers. Laurier came to believe that the best course was a cautious one. Compromise would be the key to the peaceful evolution of Canada. French and English had to work together and understand each other.

Carolus Laurier appreciated these lessons and wanted his eldest son to learn how to live with *les Anglais*. He also had great hopes for his son and knew that if one were to succeed in Canada, knowledge of the two languages and cultures was essential. When Laurier was 10, he was sent to live with an Anglo-Protestant family in New Glasgow, 11 kilometres away. Here among the Irish and Scottish immigrants, Wilfrid learned the English language and learned about the Protestant faith. He began to appreciate the English culture and began to understand that people of different backgrounds could be generous to each other. Laurier would later recall "how I fought with the Scotch boys and made schoolboy love to the Scotch girls, with more success in the latter than in the former." Remembering these days, Laurier, the politician and prime minster, would carefully develop the politics of reconciliation rather than conflict.

This was just the beginning of Laurier's education and training. In 1854, the slightly frightened boy of 13 travelled 32 kilometres to enroll in the College de l'Assomption. Founded in 1832, this was a classical college established in Quebec by the church to prepare men more for the world of God than for the world of commerce, industry and the English. Life was almost monastic here. The priests were rigid and demanding. Each student's daily schedule was set, with a great deal of time for prayer and study and only a little time for recreation. Bedtime came at eight. Laurier studied hard: Latin, the Latin classics, some pre-revolutionary French literature, Greek, a bit of English, some philosophy and history. This rigorous training was designed to prepare boys for the priesthood, although Laurier chose to study law at Montreal's McGill University.

McGill was entirely different from the College de l'Assomption. Initially, the purpose of McGill was to overwhelm the supposedly priest-ridden, ignorant and unprogressive French Canadians and impress upon them the value of assimilation. This goal had moderated by the 1860s and Laurier's class included six English and five French-Canadian students.

McGill University in the late 1860s

At McGill, Laurier was a studious, serious and dedicated young man, virtues which had been encouraged by his clerical mentors at l'Assomption. Once he determined a course of action, Laurier invariably adhered to it. Cool, dispassionate reason controlled him. He tried smoking, but when it made him ill, he quite forever. And except for the odd glass of wine with dinner, he abstained from alcohol. He was tall, over six feet, yet a bit awkward and always somewhat frail and sickly. But this had not prevented him from accomplishing his first major goal — to become a lawyer.

Near the head of his 1864 graduating class, Laurier was chosen to deliver the valedictory address. A lawyer, he stated, bore heavy responsibilities. A lawyer had to maintain liberty and justice; a lawyer had to defend the individual, especially the weak, from the bold and the strong, and that sometimes included the state and the church. Differences of language, religion or history paled in comparison to the lawyer's obligation to seek justice and freedom. These were fine words and ones which moulded the rest of Laurier's career.

Initially, that career must have been busy and exciting but also frustrating. He worked first with a small Montreal law firm. In 1866, his health and a bout of coughing blood forced him to leave the city for the backwoods of the Eastern townships. He became the editor of *Le Défricheur*, a Rouge newspaper, and settled comfortably in the small town of Victoriaville. Because of clerical opposition, *Le Défricheur* soon folded, though Laurier remained in the town to practice law. In May 1868, a doctor finally convinced Laurier that he was not going to die in the near future and with that assurance, he married Zoe Lafontaine, an attractive, talented woman who, like Laurier, had experienced the early death of a mother. At this point Laurier was content, happy with Zoe, and busy with his career.

But in nineteenth-century Quebec, an educated young man's fancy often turned to politics. This was a rapidly changing, highly politicized age. Louis-Joseph Papineau had returned from exile in 1847; Louis-Hippolyte Lafontaine and Robert Baldwin had fought for and won responsible government in 1849; Canada in the 1860s had been threatened by the United States and forced to think of its own future. That future, according to the government of the day, would depend upon the confederation of all the British North American colonies, including a very suspicious and reluctant Quebec. This union, upon which the voters were not consulted, included over two million English Canadians and only one million French Canadians. The security of the latter, along with their religion and language, did not seem guaranteed, despite the promise of provincial autonomy over cultural matters. Laurier was drawn into the battle on the side of the minority. As he had stated

Zoe Lafontaine Laurier

in his valedictory address, lawyers must protect the weak. Quebec needed men like Laurier to defend itself politically and culturally from the powerful English majority.

Chapter 2
The Young Politician

The Honourable Wilfrid Laurier M.P., a portrait taken in Ottawa in 1874

Laurier was drawn into politics somewhat reluctantly. His hesitation was due in part to his health and in part to the question of whether to join the Bleu or the Rouge party. The Bleus were led by George-Etienne Cartier and were allies of the Conservatives from Canada West under John A. Macdonald. They formed the government and endorsed Confederation. They were linked to the business elite in Canada and were supported by the powerful church establishment. At heart they were not democrats and placed little faith in the mass of the people. Yet their policies were moderate and based upon an alliance between French and English which ignored cultural and religious differences. These policies appealed to Laurier. Opposing the Bleus was the Rouge party, a group to which Laurier's father and many of his colleagues belonged. It was the party of Papineau and appealed especially to the enthusiasm of the young. Cartier was somewhat dull and pompous; the new Rouge leaders — Rodolphe Laflamme, Eric Dorion, Antoine-Aimé Dorion — were fiery and dedicated. In the 1850s, the Rouges had been democrats and idealists who wanted to introduce democracy into the Tory society which Britain had developed in Canada. They called for universal suffrage, the decentralization of political and judicial power, educational reform and the abolition of class and ecclesiastical privileges such as seigneurial dues and clerical tithes. As nationalists, the Rouges had opposed all contact with *les Anglais*, had rejected Confederation and had even suggested annexation to the United States.

These were certainly not Laurier's goals. He was much closer to the Whig, the British liberal, than to the Papineau radical. He was moderate, judicious, respectful of norms and precedents. But, by the time Laurier was ready for active politics, the Rouge party had thrown most of its youthful exuberance overboard. The Rouge leaders had ceased their strident attacks on the clergy and their flirtations with annexation. What remained attracted Laurier — a passion for individual freedom and constitutional liberty. The Rouges had even come to accept Confederation as a *fait accompli* and now were determined to make it work in Quebec's interests. That could be accomplished by ensuring that the federal government, situated in Ottawa and dominated by Ontario, respected the British North America Act. Canada's Constitution had created a federal system of government and could safeguard Quebec's linguistic and cultural autonomy.

Laurier's involvement in politics began soon after he left McGill. His law office was headed by a leading Rouge. *Le Défricheur* was a Rouge newspaper and Laurier's predecessor as editor had been Eric Dorion. By 1871, the Rouge party had recognized Laurier's talents and had prevailed upon him to contest a seat in the provincial election of that year. Running in the constituency of Drummond-Arthabaska, Laurier easily wrested the seat from its Conservative incumbent, Edward Hemmings. The fact that the Rouge party was swamped elsewhere in the province made Laurier's victory all the more impressive.

In the Assembly, Laurier soon made his mark by effectively arguing against the current system of dual representation. This system permitted an individual to sit in both the provincial Assembly and the federal House of Commons. It compensated for the dearth of high-calibre politicians, but it also permitted the federal party to control the local one. Laurier, like the Liberals in Ontario, condemned dual representation since it encouraged the mixing of federal and provincial concerns. The division of powers as laid down in the British North America Act and the principle of provincial autonomy would become mere shams if dual representation continued. Laurier made his point forcefully: "With the single mandate, Quebec is Quebec; with the double mandate, it becomes merely an appendix to Ottawa."

*The Pacific Scandal brought
criticism from every segment
of the population.*

The Conservative majority in the Quebec Assembly disagreed
with Laurier and rejected his motion. However, his arguments,
evolving as they did from his constitutional and legal training, were
essentially sound. In 1872, Ontario abolished the practice and in
1873, the Dominion Parliament made provincial M.L.A.'s ineligible
for seats in the federal house. Laurier had been vindicated and had
made an auspicious debut on the political scene. But Laurier was not,
at this stage, the most energetic of individuals. In fact, lethargic
might not be too harsh a description. Throughout his career he had
to be pushed — into marriage, into provincial politics, into federal
politics, into the cabinet. He was often caught up in events rather
than in control of them.

In 1873, events again carried Laurier along. On November 5, John A. Macdonald offered his government's resignation to the governor general, Lord Dufferin, who had to accept because of the Pacific Scandal. Conservative leaders had been receiving, for election purposes, large sums of money from a railway-man who at the same time was bidding for an important government contract. This blatant conflict of interest was just too much for the Canadian public to tolerate and the Liberal party, led by Alexander Mackenzie, formed the new administration. Mackenzie soon called a general election, and in February 1874, the Liberals were returned with a large majority. One of the new members, elected from Drummond-Arthabaska and urged into the election by his friends, was the young Wilfrid Laurier.

In March 1874, Laurier moved to the Russell Hotel in Ottawa. He was a bit lonely — Zoe had remained in Quebec — and frightened. In fact, he avoided the governor general's soiree for M.P.'s because of his insecurity. He was awed and overwhelmed by the people around him. There was Mackenzie, the dour Scot from Sarnia whom chance had brought to power. There was Edward Blake, whose towering intellect and aloof manner intimidated everyone including the new prime minister. Across the floor in Parliament was Sir John A. Macdonald himself, somewhat humbled by the scandal but still an impressive figure. It was in this atmosphere that Laurier made his first speech as an M.P., a speech which was ignored by most of the members because it was delivered in French.

However, Laurier was soon caught up in the business of Parliament. The first major concern of the House of Commons involved Louis Riel and the Manitoba rebellion of 1870. In 1869, the government of Canada had purchased the western territories from the Hudson's Bay Company and then set out to quickly integrate the area into the rest of the country. But the transfer of power had not been peaceful. The Métis in Manitoba, ably led by Louis Riel, had refused to be bought like a piece of prairie sod and had turned to armed resistance. But the Métis rebellion ended once the Canadian government granted them guarantees for their land, language and culture.

By 1874, Manitoba was peaceful but Ottawa was not. The Mackenzie government had not finished with the Métis question because there was still an outstanding warrant and $5,000 reward for the elusive Riel. Riel had been elected to the House of Commons from Manitoba and in January 1874, in the company of a French-Canadian M.P., had entered Parliament and had been sworn in by the clerk of the House. He then disappeared again. Meanwhile, one of Riel's lieutenants, Ambroise Lépine, had been captured, tried and

Louis Riel (centre) and his council, 1869-1870

sentenced to death.

In January 1875, Lord Dufferin intervened in Lépine's case, commuting his sentence to two years in prison and a permanent loss of civil rights. The Mackenzie government, feeling the need to placate Quebec and be rid of this issue, turned to the larger and more contentious problem of Riel himself and moved that he be pardoned.

Laurier spoke on this resolution with sincerity and emotion. Apologizing for his awkwardness, he spoke in English to all of Canada. His French background, Laurier said, made him sympathize with Riel and the Métis. But his knowledge of British justice and fair play also made him feel that Riel had not been treated fairly in the past. Parliament now had to rectify the situation and get on with issues that concerned the future, not the past. After much debate, Parliament agreed and on a vote of 126 to 50, Riel was granted a pardon conditional on five years of exile.

The new, inexperienced and quickly exhausted Liberal government concentrated on other, equally important legislative measures. But these new laws were aimed at long-term effects and failed to drum up any immediate electoral enthusiasm. The Liberals introduced the secret ballot and ended the practice whereby elections were spread over weeks or months. They passed a strong Corrupt

Practices Act and transferred the settlement of disputed elections from Parliament to the apolitical courts. They established the Royal Military College in Kingston and the North West Mounted Police and passed the Scott Act providing for the prohibition of liquor in counties which desired to be dry. Finally, the Liberal party began the process of reassessing Canada's colonial status by establishing the Supreme Court of Canada and by restricting the independent powers of the governor general.

All these issues struck a responsive chord in Laurier, though he was not always active in the debates. However, his true worth to the Liberals emerged in another issue, this one involving Quebec, the province which was and always would be Laurier's power base. As the new leader of the Liberal party's Quebec wing and a prospective cabinet minister, Laurier was called upon to do battle with the Roman Catholic hierarchy in Quebec. This battle had to take place, in spite of Laurier's desire for compromise, if the Liberals were to make gains in that province.

Laurier had to confront two bishops, Ignace Bourget of Montreal and Louis Laflèche of Trois-Rivières, and their adherence to ultramontanism. Bourget was the major problem because of his immense popularity in the province. In 1837, he alone among the hierarchy had befriended the Patriotes and then, after being named a bishop in 1840, had undertaken a host of charitable works. His philosophy, ultramontanism, was international in scope and was a fiercely conservative reaction to the gains made by liberals, "atheists" and secularists in Europe throughout the nineteenth century. Ultramontanism urged acceptance of the status quo and tried to prevent any questioning of the conventions and attitudes of the time. It was an attempt to restore order, to confirm the infallibility of the Pope and to define, by means of the *Index*, just what Catholics could and could not read. It was an attempt to ensure that Catholics did not associate with Protestants and, in Quebec, to ensure that Catholics did not vote for Liberals, whom Bourget considered anti-clerical revolutionaries. Ultramontanes like Bourget and Laflèche were intolerant, dogmatic individuals who would go to almost any length to impose their narrow view of society on Quebec. They could not understand that a country such as Canada had to be based upon tolerance.

By 1877, Laurier already had a backlog of personal experiences with the ultramontanes. His father had always been somewhat independent of the church and had earned his priest's enmity by sending young Wilfrid to live with a Protestant family. That was considered fraternization with the enemy. Laurier, while in Montreal, had felt the ultramontane bludgeon himself. Like many

Bishop Ignace Bourget

other young liberals, he was active in the Institut Canadien, a study and discussion group. This association enraged Bourget because it had Protestant members and because it ignored the censorship imposed by the *Index*. Eventually, Bourget effectively closed the Institut by threatening to excommunicate its members. Another confrontation with ultramontanism came in Victoriaville. There Bishop Laflèche and the parish priest verbally attacked Laurier's newspaper, *Le Défricheur*, because of its Rouge orientation. The paper lost its subscribers and closed its offices.

Now Laurier had to confront the church again because Bourget, Laflèche, archbishop Taschereau of Quebec City and most of the lower clergy refused to believe that Canadian Liberals such as Laurier were not the anti-clerical liberals of continental Europe. The clerics condemned the Liberal party and prevented their parishioners from voting for its candidates.

On the night of June 26, 1877, Laurier, speaking in Quebec City, made his most memorable speech. Calling upon all his experience and eloquence, he defined the principles of Liberalism in order to dispel the clergy's incorrect notion that Liberalism meant heresy in faith and revolution in politics. To Laurier, Liberalism meant gradual reform along the lines of the British model, reform which prevented revolution. He admitted that in the 1840s the Rouges had been radicals. But times had changed. The Rouges had been young then and were older now. He stressed that to condemn the Liberal party was to endorse blindly the Conservative party regardless of how corrupt or intellectually bankrupt it might be at any particular moment. And to suggest, as Bourget had, the formation of a purely Catholic party in a mixed country such as Canada was wrong and dangerous. The consequence would be the formation of a Protestant party which would throw "open the door to war, a war of religion, the most terrible of wars." Laurier ended with a plea that the clergy respect both the elector's independence and his right to choose between two parties. Intimidation, intolerance, and rigid dogmatism had no place in Laurier's Canada.

His speech had been courageous and electrifying. It did not settle the issue entirely — indeed the question of the church's role in politics would remain controversial until the 1890s when again Laurier would be intimately involved. But this speech, along with the Pope's own intervention, did oblige the Quebec hierarchy to ease up some. In October 1877, the bishops met and issued a new pastoral which declared that no political party was condemned. In an accompanying circular, priests were forbidden to teach that it was a sin to vote for a particular party or candidate. The Liberals in Quebec were ecstatic and hailed Laurier for his part in their victory.

But life was not to be that simple for Laurier. He was taken into the Mackenzie cabinet in the fall of 1877 and, consequently, had to be re-elected in Drummond-Arthabaska. This was a bothersome practice, necessary for everyone who accepted a cabinet portfolio and often merely a formality. But it became more than that in Laurier's case because the province's ultramontanes, laymen this time, were bitter and angry. They vowed to destroy Laurier and did succeed in defeating him. When the ballots were counted, Laurier had lost by 24 votes. Violence, intimidation, slander and bribery had taken their toll.

Laurier was crestfallen and once again physically ill, worn out by the campaign. By early November though, he was back in the fray running in the constituency of Quebec East. This campaign was also violent and corrupt, though this time the Liberals were equally guilty. Laurier won this election with a respectable majority of over 300 votes. He was back in the House of Commons, and Quebec East would be his political home for the next 40 years.

Chapter 3
Prelude to Power

Laurier was now back in Alexander Mackenzie's cabinet. Another general election was slated for September 1878 and the Liberals felt some degree of confidence. The government had ben honest and reasonably efficient; it had introduced several important pieces of legislation. But still it was in trouble with the electorate because the Liberal leaders had tried to be statesmen, not politicians. For the most part they were principled, sometimes dogmatic men who ignored and rejected the compromises so necessary in politics. Their rigidity had offended several important groups. In addition, the government was divided, weakened by retirements and unable to give effective leadership during a period of serious economic depression. Laurier was enough of a realist to suspect that the party would be swept from office in September. "Our party," he wrote to one acquaintance, "is going to the dogs."

Laurier was prophetic. The electorate had a short memory and John A. Macdonald, now fully recovered from the scandal of 1873, was at his captivating best promising a bit for everyone. For Westerners, for manufacturers, indeed for all Canadians weary of economic depression and lackluster Liberals, he promised a new National Policy. This three-fold policy involved tariff protection for Canadian industry, a transcontinental railway linking the West and the East, and immigrants to populate the West. These immigrants would make the Canadian Pacific Railway profitable and would provide a large consumer market for the industries fostered by the tariff. This platform, although too simplistic and optimistic, sounded good. It promised Canadian economic independence; it promised prosperity; it gave Canadians something exciting to believe in.

The Liberals, on the other hand, promised nothing new and the voters responded by rejecting them. Laurier, after exactly one year in office, now embarked upon 18 frustrating years in the Opposition. He found those years disagreeable because he wanted to accomplish things himself, not merely criticize what other people did. But this election marked a turning point in Laurier's political education. He began to appreciate the importance of style and charisma in a leader. He also began to appreciate the necessity of political compromise.

THE OLD FLAG.
THE OLD POLICY,
THE OLD LEADER.

Macdonald returned to power with a National Policy which promised something for everyone.

He felt a politician must have definite goals — in his case, national unity — but to achieve anything, a politician had to remain in office. One could be moralistic, rigid and uncompromising in the Opposition, but what did that actually accomplish? Laurier began to see that true power depended on being in office. Once in office, he

Prelude to Power

Alexander Mackenzie

must do anything to stay there in order to bring about the unity and harmony he so desperately desired for Canada.

To improve its chances in the next election, the Liberal caucus, in April 1880, decided to select a new leader. Laurier was one of the five M.P.'s who carried the news to the bitter and coldly formal Mackenzie. It was an onerous task for Laurier, but politically necessary. However, the party's new leader, Edward Blake, was hardly better. He was a fine individual — absolutely honest, principled and brilliant — but he was not a politician who could compete with Sir John A. Macdonald. Blake was thin-skinned and difficult to approach. There was none of that easy rapport with other M.P.'s or with the electorate that so character-ized Sir John A. Nor was Blake an ambitious politician who would capitalize on every mistake made by his opponents.

Perhaps most destructive to the Liberals was Blake's inability to make political compromises. He tried valiantly to adhere to his personal principles but could never appreciate the political damage he was doing. He criticized specific tariffs when tariffs in general were still popular with the electorate. He criticized the cost of the CPR when the electorate was still mesmerized by its scope. He spoke of restraint when the electorate wanted grandiose schemes which would fulfill Canada's manifest destiny. As a result of Blake's political deficiencies and the party's shortcomings, Macdonald was able, on two occasions, to "wrest victory from the jaws of defeat." The Conservatives' National Policy had not been successful, and the Liberals could have won or certainly should have done better during the elections of 1882 and 1887 — but they did not.

Laurier, as leader of the Quebec wing of the party, was partially responsible for these successive defeats. In Parliament he appeared

Laurier's country home in Arthabaskaville, P.Q., was a common meeting ground for French-Canadian politicians.

lazy, a once bright light that had faded. The impression, however, was not quite fair since Laurier was busy learning from those around him how to be a successful politician. He watched Edward Blake and noted his faults. He watched the cunning and ever appealing Macdonald and copied his strengths.

Outside Parliament, Laurier busied himself building a political organization in Quebec. In 1882, he was elected mayor of Arthabaskaville. In the summer of 1883, he conducted Blake and Richard Cartwright, another leading Liberal, on a speaking tour through Montreal and the Eastern Townships of Quebec. He attended every banquet or gathering he could and spoke to whatever audience invited him. His rather grand home in Arthabaskaville was a popular meeting place for Rouge and Bleu politicians alike. All these contracts could prove invaluable to the party and, later, to himself. Blake had always ignored the party organization and grass roots, but Macdonald did not and Laurier would not.

Prelude to Power

Laurier was also learning how to attack political opponents and capitalize on their shortcomings. In 1881, he brought his new style to the public via the pages of *L'Electeur*, a mudslinging Liberal newspaper founded in Quebec City one year earlier. In an unsigned article entitled "The Den of Forty Thieves," Laurier unleashed a vicious attack on several Conservative leaders in Quebec, accusing them of gross corruption. When the accused responded with a $100,000 libel suit, Laurier identified himself as the author. Lengthy arguments in court resulted in a hung jury, and the trial ended with the provincial Conservatives tarnished and Liberals throughout the province rejoicing at their own success and at Laurier's new enthusiasm.

But Laurier did not carry his enthusiasm into the House of Commons. Perhaps the House was less important than the hustings for political success. Still, if Laurier were to make his mark nationally, he would have to impress his parliamentary colleagues. This he did only sporadically. One of the key issues to shake Canada throughout this period was the tariff. Its existence or the level at which it was set was of crucial importance to Canada's industrial and national development. Yet Laurier simply was not interested. He was a lawyer, not a businessman or banker.

Laurier's performance improved when other issues were involved, issues which touched upon his interest in the Constitution or in minority rights. One such question, the Letellier affair, arose soon after the Liberal government's defeat in 1878. It involved the right of the federal government to interfere with the autonomy of the provinces.

In March 1878, Luc Letellier de Saint-Just, the lieutenant-governor of Quebec and a prominent Rouge, had dismissed the local Conservative administration for incompetence. He then called upon the provincial Liberals to form the government. To the federal Conservatives, this was the most outrageous political interference imaginable. However, the new provincial government, under Henri Joli, had been re-elected by the voters after the summer election campaign.

When the federal Conservatives regained office in the fall of 1878, the Quebec members moved that Letellier be censured and removed from office. Their resolution passed by a substantial majority, but not before Laurier had spoken out as the guardian of provincial autonomy. In his speech Laurier stressed not Letellier's actions, but the fact that the people of Quebec themselves had not objected. Since they were satisfied, the Dominion government had no right to interfere. Laurier asserted that interference in such cases would be a violation of the federal principle and would be jeopardizing provincial independence for the sake of political revenge. Provincial autonomy, whether in the 1870s or the 1890s, was something Laurier cherished.

Another issue which touched Laurier involved minority rights. Considering his French-Canadian background, it was only natural that minority rights would have moved him to action. The shortcomings of the Macdonald government on the resurgent issue of Métis rights provided Laurier with an excellent opportunity to defend a cause, to score political points and to restore the political reputation he had enjoyed when he first entered Parliament. Louis Riel and the North West Rebellion of 1885 were godsends for Wilfrid Laurier, the politician.

Basically, the Métis were struggling to survive in a changing environment and, for many, starvation was a distinct possibility. Financially tight-fisted and concerned with other issues, the government completely ignored repeated and urgent appeals for aid

Edward Blake

from the Métis and Native peoples. Eventually, Louis Riel, now given to bouts of emotional instability, returned from exile to lead his people in what began as a peaceful struggle and ended as a rebellion. Only at this point did an alarmed and vengeful government respond. Troops were dispatched, the insurrection was quelled and Louis Riel, after an unfair trial and agonizing months in prison, was executed.

In Parliament the Liberal Opposition seized on this issue. Blake spoke at great length, but it was Laurier, at his eloquent best, who captured the attention and admiration of the House. This time, though, it seemed to be partisan politics rather than principle that motivated Laurier. He, like all of Quebec, was drawn to Riel by language and religion, but at the same time he did not want to offend Liberal voters in Ontario. In an impassioned speech which appealed to Quebec but did not alienate Ontario, Laurier attacked not Riel but the Macdonald government for oppressing a proud people. Drawing analogies to Papineau and the Rebellion of 1837, he insisted that an oppressed people have no choice but to rise up. Treat a group fairly and they will be satisfied. Meet their needs, at least partially, and they will respond generously. Respect British standards of fair play and justice, and the minority will remain loyal. The government, Laurier claimed, had done none of these. It was the government and not Riel which was to blame for the rebellion and for the subsequent English-French antagonisms which threatened Confederation itself.

With a comfortable majority backing him, Macdonald survived this attack, but the Liberal party — and Laurier especially — gained ground. During the 1887 federal election and for the first time since 1874, the Liberals won half the seats in Quebec. Power eluded them, however, because Ontario failed to vote Liberal. Following the election, the petulant Blake resigned as the party's leader and nominated Laurier as his successor. Laurier hesitated because of poor health and his usual lack of enthusiasm, while the party leaders worried about Ontario's reaction to a French-Catholic leader. But Blake still wielded considerable influence and Laurier was named his successor.

Laurier did not lead the Liberals out of the political wilderness immediately — both he and the party had to endure one more significant electoral defeat. In the 1891 election, Laurier, still uncertain of himself in Ontario, relied upon Richard Cartwright for a bold, new campaign issue — unrestricted reciprocity, or free trade, with the United States. However, Sir John A., the crafty old politician, effectively convinced the voters that this supposedly economic union would lead inevitably to political union and the demise of Canada as a British nation.

This emotional tactic won Macdonald yet another majority, but a majority that differed from previous ones: Nova Scotia, New Brunswick and the western provinces and territories voted overwhelmingly Conservative; Quebec went Liberal by a narrow margin of nine; Ontario divided its seats almost equally, 48 for the Conservatives and 44 for the Liberals. Laurier appreciated the significance of this. To become prime minister, all he had to do was to expand his political base in Quebec while holding onto the support he had in Ontario.

Before long, the Manitoba government of Thomas Greenway, another Liberal, made this possible. In Manitoba, French Catholics had always enjoyed a publicly supported system of denominational and French-language schools. In 1891, Greenway halted funds for these schools and effectively abolished them. Franco-Manitoban and Québécois communities protested immediately because both the British North America Act and the 1870 Manitoba Act seemingly protected these schools.

The issue progressed through the courts until finally the Privy Council in Britain, the final court of appeal for the colonies, ruled that the federal government had a right to pass remedial legislation which would restore the separate school system. This proved to be an incredibly divisive issue. Ontario in general did not wish to see Manitoba coerced by federal legislation and did not believe that French Catholics should have special privileges. Quebec generally felt just the opposite.

It is possible that John A. Macdonald, the old compromiser, could have resolved this issue to the satisfaction of most, but he had died after the strenuous 1891 campaign. His successors, four in five years, were not as capable as he. All grappled with the question of remedial legislation and succeeded only in dividing both their party and the country. Eventually, a Liberal filibuster forced a federal election during which Conservative leader, Sir Charles Tupper, promised remedial legislation. His position was politically viable. In the once Conservative stronghold of Quebec, he could pose as the defender of French-Canadian rights and receive the hearty endorsement of the clerical leaders. In Ontario, he could appeal to the strong British ties of the electorate by claiming that he did not like coercing Manitoba, but the Privy Council had made its decision and he was compelled to obey. Besides, he asked, whom do you trust, a French Catholic like Laurier or an Anglo-Protestant like myself?

Unlike past elections however, the Conservatives were not fighting political weaklings. Laurier had grown in confidence and now was an excellent campaigner. The Liberal party was for once united and for the first time strong in all parts of the country. The trade question, so deadly in the past, had been dropped by the Liberal party at its 1893 national convention.

Laurier was torn by the Manitoba schools question. As a French Catholic, he wished to see Catholic rights restored and minorities respected, but as a strict constitutionalist, he did not wish to see the federal government coercing a province and interfering in what was a provincial realm of jurisdiction, namely education. However, feeling power to be within his grasp, Laurier took the middle of the road. He would try to outflank all those who adhered dogmatically to either side of the argument.

Laurier and the Liberals opted for compromise. In Quebec, he stressed the crucial issue of provincial autonomy and claimed that through compromise he would do what he could for the minority. Liberals in Quebec reversed the Conservatives' tactics and asked, whom do you trust, a French Catholic or an Anglo-Protestant? They emphasized how gratifying it would be to have a French-Canadian prime minister. Laurier played upon his own natural appeal in Quebec and in the end swept the province, winning 49 of its 65 seats.

In Ontario meanwhile, Laurier was very cautious. His supporters condemned the Conservatives for trying to legislate "special rights" and for attempting to coerce a province in order to woo the Roman Catholic Church in Quebec. Ironically, it was Laurier, a French Canadian, who posed as the defender not of the minority but of the aggressive majority. Laurier's approach was politically perfect — the Liberals won 43 of 86 seats which, added to the Quebec seats and a number from the other parts of Canada, were enough to bring them to power for the first time in almost two decades.

The Liberals and Laurier were ecstatic and the lessons of 1896 were not soon forgotten. Indeed these lessons — the importance of preserving Quebec as a power base and the need to compromise principles — would keep Laurier in office for 15 years, the longest uninterrupted term of office for any prime minister either before or since.

Chapter 4
An Autonomous Colony

On July 13, 1896, Wilfrid Laurier became the first French-Canadian prime minister of Canada. He brought a great deal of style and grace to the office. At 55, he was quite handsome. His thinning hair was fashionably done; his suits, vests and hats were almost elegant; his style was courteous, gracious and endearing.

Zoe Laurier was less comfortable in her new surroundings. She had remained the small town girl who enjoyed gardening and entertaining neighbourhood children more than she enjoyed politics or the limelight of power. As a result, Laurier developed a very close relationship with the wife of another Arthabaskaville lawyer. Emilie Lavergne, more so than Zoe, met the tastes of the new prime minister. Emilie had toured Paris and London; she was well-read, fashionable and refined; she was determined to teach Laurier the etiquette which would permit him to mingle with society's leaders. There was always a great deal of gossip about their relationship, especially since the Laurier marriage was childless. But gossip never deterred either of them. They spent many quiet afternoons together, and when Laurier was in Ottawa, the two corresponded regularly and warmly.

Emilie Lavergne

Hon. Sir Louis H. Davies, M.P.,
Minister of Marine and Fisheries.

Hon. W. S. Fielding, M.P.,
Minister of Finance.

Hon. A. G. Blair, M.P.,
Minister of Railways and Canals.

Hon. Clifford Sifton, M.P.,
Minister of the Interior.

Rt. Hon. Sir Wilfrid Laurier, G.C.M.G., M.P.,
Prime Minister and President of the Council.

Hon. J. I. Tarte, M.P.,
Minister of Public Works.

Hon. David Mills, Senate,
Minister of Justice.

Hon. Wm. Mullock, M.P.,
Postmaster General.

Hon. Sir Richard Cartwright,
G.C.M.G., M.P.,
Minister of Trade and Commerce.

*A lithograph showing the
1899 Liberal cabinet*

With almost paternal concern, Laurier always enquired about Emilie's son. The boy, who reminded Laurier of himself in so many ways, was clever, quick-witted and a bit lazy. Laurier never did ask about her daughter or husband and only rarely mentioned Zoe. Yet if Zoe was concerned about this relationship, she never showed it. Emilie was her friend as well.

Laurier's new position was welcomed by Zoe in one way — for the first time in their marriage, they would be financially secure. The office did not pay well, but Laurier's admirers did. After the election, a group of them offered to raise between $50,000 and $100,000 for his personal use. Laurier gratefully accepted the offer since there were no strings attached. John A. Macdonald had had a similar fund at his disposal, a fund which ensured that he could remain in politics permanently. The Liberal party, also grateful to Laurier, added its own gift of a very pleasant house in Ottawa, not far from Parliament Hill.

With these matters settled, Laurier could devote his time to forming a cabinet. He did not take direct responsibility for any department because he wanted to be free to look after the party's organization, especially in Quebec, and to be involved in any department which interested him. Laurier rarely needed to interfere in his colleagues' activities, however, because he had chosen excellent men. By 1896, he understood the forces that characterized Canada and represented each of these forces in his cabinet. From Quebec, he selected both Liberals and old Blues such as Israel Tarte. In the Liberal-Conservative tradition of George-Etienne Cartier, Laurier became a middle-of-the-road moderate, a position which would ensure political success in Quebec. And Laurier was so confident of his own ability to assess public opinion in that province that he would not permit any Quebec minister to rival his own power.

Once Quebec was taken care of, Laurier turned his attention to the rest of the country. He had always believed in provincial autonomy and appreciated Canadians' strong identification with their own region or province. Laurier earnestly wished to build a new nationalist commitment among Canadians, but the way to accomplish this was to recognize the old regional loyalties. Therefore, he brought strong representatives from each region into his cabinet.

One was Oliver Mowat, the elderly and extremely popular premier of Ontario. Others were W.S. Fielding, premier of Nova Scotia, and A.G. Blair, premier of New Brunswick. Clifford Sifton, a Manitoba cabinet minister, was brought to Ottawa to direct western development. Anglophones in Quebec, Irish Catholics in Ontario, manufacturers, farmers, bankers — all had their strong cabinet which would try to satisfy the needs of all Canadians.

The first issue for the new government was the still unresolved Manitoba schools question. Laurier, during the campaign, had promised "sunny ways" — the use of gentle persuasion rather than active intervention. This is precisely what Manitoba got. Instead of threatening coercive legislation, Laurier corresponded amicably with Thomas Greenway and dispatched federal emissaries to Winnipeg. By 1897, they had agreed upon a compromise which recognized the principle of non-denominational schools but which still gave important concessions to the French-Catholic minority.

The Laurier-Greenway agreement met with general approval. It was not everything that the Catholics had demanded, but neither was it everything that the Manitoba government or the Orange Order in Ontario had insisted upon earlier. It was a compromise with all the defects inherent in such arrangements, but it could be tolerated. Most Canadians, with the exception of several Catholic bishops, were only too glad to see the issue brought to an end.

Laurier and his "sunny ways" were off to a good start. As prime minister he had a clear idea of what he wished to accomplish. "My object," Laurier wrote to a friend in 1904, "is to consolidate Confederation, and to bring our people long estranged from each other, gradually to become a nation. This is the supreme issue.

"HOME, SWEET HOME."

Everything else is subordinate to that idea." While the composition of his cabinet reflected this goal by accommodating regional differences, the historic differences between French and English Canadians were more difficult to deal with. These two national groups had separate visions of Canada and each sought a different destiny for the country as a whole.

The task of accommodating the two groups would be difficult, but Laurier felt it was possible if he were able to remain in office. Laurier, like all prime ministers, felt that he could serve the country as no rival could. He planned to stay in office for the longest possible time in order to devote himself to reconciliation and compromise. By monopolizing the middle of the road, he would attract the support of most moderate Canadians, leaving the extremists, whether French or English, out in the cold. Canadian unity would rest on his shoulders.

However, national unity was as difficult to develop in this era as in any other. Perhaps it was even more difficult because of the divisive issue of Canada's relationship with Great Britain and the empire. Generally, English Canadians wanted to strengthen the bonds between the various parts of the empire, and emotionally, imperialism struck a responsive chord. Many Canadians had only recently come to this country, and to them membership in a close-knit empire enhanced Canada's own importance and prestige. Alone, Canada was a small, underpopulated, rather insignificant country living in the shadow of the United States; as part of the empire, Canada could share in England's strength and glory.

French Canadians simply did not fit into the ambitious schemes of the imperialists. They were supposedly backward, unprogressive, priest-ridden and, as Catholics, disloyal citizens, owing their first allegiance to the Pope of Rome rather than the Queen of England. There was a certain irony in this last criticism, for the French Canadians, unlike their English compatriots, had been settled in Canada since the seventeenth century. They perceived themselves as the only true Canadians, giving their undivided loyalty to Canada while Anglo-Canadians divided their loyalty between homeland and mother country.

The French Canadians were as resolute in their anti-imperialist stance as English Canadians were in their imperialism. Laurier, a moderate on this question, was the political chief of the French Canadians, but on the issue of imperialism, Henri Bourassa surpassed him in popular appeal. Bourassa, the grandson of Louis-Joseph Papineau and the young M.P. from Terrebonne, was a brilliant, idealistic and committed

Henri Bourassa

individual. He wanted a Canada based upon equal rights for French and English, and it was Bourassa who popularized the notion of Confederation as a compact between the two founding cultures. When speaking of Canada's internal affairs, he idealized the notion of provincial autonomy. In international politics, he idealized the notion of Canadian autonomy within the empire.

Bourassa and Laurier shared a common opinion on these matters but with a sharp difference. Laurier was a practicing politician, committed to retaining power and willing to make whatever compromises were necessary to accomplish that goal. Laurier understood that a politician could not be dogmatic on any issue but had to reach a position between two extremes. Bourassa, even though an M.P., was not a politician at heart; he was an idealist. His political philosophy was noble but politically impractical. "To govern," he

A Diamond Jubilee portrait of Queen Victoria

wrote, "is to have the courage, at a given moment, to risk power to save a principle."

Laurier would never risk power. To accommodate English Canadians, he praised Canada's ties to the empire and devoted himself to British principles; to appease French Canadians, he declared that Canada was autonomous within the empire. He was very much the political pragmatist. He had much to accomplish and had to stay in office to do so.

In 1897, Laurier and Zoe travelled to England to participate in the festivities surrounding Queen Victoria's Diamond Jubilee. As the leader of Britain's senior self- governing dominion and as an elegant, eloquent individual, Laurier attracted a great deal of attention. He was invited to numerous banquets and delivered many speeches; he participated in the magnificent Jubilee pageant; he reviewed the mighty British fleet at Spithead; he received honorary degrees from Oxford and Cambridge; he was a guest at Windsor Castle and Buckingham Palace; he was knighted by the Queen herself. He had not sought this last honour, for it offended his liberal sensibilities; but Sir Wilfrid Laurier, the leader of a once conquered people, accepted.

Much of the attention lavished on Laurier and other colonial leaders had been orchestrated by Joseph Chamberlain, the colonial secretary in the British government. Chamberlain was firmly committed not only to the idea of empire but also to certain practical schemes for integrating more fully its various members. He wanted a free trade arrangement among them, a single navy, paid for by all, as well as an imperial council to oversee imperial affairs. Chamberlain was so narrow-minded and self-centred that he failed to realize that these measures were of primary benefit to England, not to the colonies. The empire was not a partnership or a commonwealth of nations; it was an association which England dominated and guided for its own well-being.

Laurier, though flattered by the attention and honours, was not overwhelmed by them. Even while in England, he remained neither imperialist nor anti-imperialist, but a politician appealing to all factions. For the English, for Chamberlain and for the most rabid English Canadians, he made several important speeches in which he seemed to endorse Chamberlain's goals and the imperialist line. Canada, he stated, would always be ready to strengthen its ties with England.

However, while flattering the English, Laurier knew that his most important audience was in Quebec and Canada. He avoided Canadian commitments to the empire because such commitments would prove unpopular back home. Laurier remained very cautious on imperialist issues throughout the series of colonial conferences held in 1897, 1902, 1903 and 1907. He insisted, though usually discreetly, that he opposed any formalization of the existing imperial ties. He maintained that Canada's obligations to the empire must remain undefined and that the extent of Canada's contribution must be decided in Canada, by Canadians, and according to Canadian needs. Canadians would do their part to strengthen the empire by strengthening Canada itself, by making it prosperous, by developing its resources and potential.

Laurier clearly supported Canadian autonomy though for domestic political reasons he did not parade his feelings as openly as did Henri Bourassa. In Laurier's mind, imperial commitments might retard Canadian development while certainly provoking cultural and political disharmony. And Canada's development, not England's problems, was his major concern. Laurier's thoughts on imperialism and his ability to compromise were soon put to the test. In October 1899, England went to war against the Boers in South Africa, supposedly to protect the interests of the British minority living there. Joseph Chamberlain issued a call for Canadian troops to fight with the British, and in general, English Canadians responded positively. Here was an opportunity to prove the unity and strength of the empire. Here also was an opportunity to exhibit Canada's maturity and to repay Britain for its aid and protection in the past.

The French Canadians, however, opposed Canadian participation with equal vehemence. Led by Henri Bourassa, they

The Ottawa railway station on Jan. 20, 1900, when "D" Battery, Second Canadian Contingent, left for South Africa

identified with the Boers, as suppressed people, and denounced all empires as corrupt, repressive and hateful. They passionately urged Canadian abstention from this imperialist war.

Laurier faced a considerable dilemma, since he would be condemned by one of the two sides no matter what policy he followed. After heated cabinet meetings, Laurier devised a plan which would satisfy almost everyone. The government would equip and transport a purely volunteer force of 1,000 men. Once in South Africa, the British government would assume financial and political responsibility for them.

Politically, Laurier's stand was an extremely shrewd compromise. In Quebec, he could stress that participation was voluntary, that the government had given only minimal assistance and that this action would not set any precedents for the future. In Ontario and the rest of English Canada, he could pose as a true loyalist who had responded to England's needs.

Not everyone was satisfied, of course. Some English Canadian nationalists criticized Laurier for not insisting upon independent Canadian participation. Some imperialists criticized Laurier for not doing enough, even though by the end of the war over 7,000 Canadians fought the Boers. And some French Canadians criticized

An Autonomous Colony

Laurier for doing too much. Bourassa resigned his House of Commons seat in protest and then ran again on an anti-imperialist platform.

Bourassa was re-elected by acclamation. Laurier had not run a Liberal against him because he wanted to appease both Bourassa and Quebec. Appeasement was obviously the key to the prime minister's policy. French and English Canada had split on a critical issue, and Laurier had compromised in the interest of national unity. He had attempted to avoid an irreparable split in Canada and, as the election of 1900 proved, he had succeeded. Quebec, in spite of Bourassa, gave Laurier 57 of its 65 seats; English Canada gave him over half its seats.

Laurier's ability to compromise on the imperial question was soon tested again. During various colonial conferences, Britain had urged the creation of an imperial navy, to which all the colonies would contribute men and money. Laurier had resisted this issue because it was not one of Canada's own priorities and because it would seriously divide Canada. He also realized, as Bourassa did, that it would remain, in spite of what it was called, a British navy. It would protect British trade routes, British interests and British shores. It might protect Canada too but only indirectly since Canada had no overseas enemies. Canada's one possible enemy was the United States and a British navy certainly would be of no use in any struggle with that continental giant.

Laurier's arguments held sway until 1908, when England and Germany became involved in an intense race for naval supremacy. England appealed to the colonies for contributions, and this time English Canada responded vigorously. The mother country, it was argued, was in real danger and needed the aid which Canada could now afford to give. The French-Canadian response, still moulded by Bourassa, was one of alarm and fierce opposition. French Canadians wanted greater Canadian independence and argued that contributions to an imperial navy would drag the country into a European power struggle and perhaps war.

Wilfrid Laurier, now accustomed to dealing with such polarized opponents, attempted once again to find a moderate, middle-of-the-road position which would appeal to all but the most extreme. On January 12, 1910, he presented Parliament with his Naval Service Bill, which he felt was a reasonable compromise. Canada would develop its own navy, its own naval reserves and its own naval college. To appease Quebec, these would remain under Canadian control and would serve Canadian needs. To appease English Canada, the bill provided that in time of war and with Parliament's consent, Canada's naval resources could be placed under imperial control.

An Autonomous Colony

First Canadian Navy recruiting poster, 1911

After a lengthy and emotional debate, Parliament passed the measure and Canada had, as one critic complained, its own "tin pot navy." Two aging British cruisers, the *Rainbow* and *Niobe*, were to be Canada's contribution to imperial defence. This time though, Laurier, in spite of his best efforts, had appeased neither the moderates nor the extremists. The naval issue would continue to convulse Canada for some years yet.

The decade-long imperial debate had exposed Laurier's character and his tactics. He was an ambitious politician who could not survive without support from both English and French Canadians. Since their views on imperialism were diametrically opposed, he was obliged to remain flexible, moderate and open to all possibilities. Intransigence and idealism were political liabilities and had no place in his attitudes or tactics. Behind Laurier's actions was a concept of Canada's destiny. The empire's strength, he felt, rested upon British principles, not upon aggressive imperialism. The empire's strength depended upon local diversity and freedom. Canada was a willing member of the empire, but its contributions would depend upon the priorities, the abilities and the loyalties of Canadians themselves.

Chapter 5
A Prosperous Nation

Though the imperial question consumed much of Sir Wilfrid Laurier's attention while prime minister, his foremost concern was with Canada itself, its prosperity, its development and its destiny. Laurier was a lucky man. Throughout his life, he had often been pushed into the right place at the right time. The consequence had been power, prestige and a comfortable degree of fortune. In 1896 and after, circumstances again collaborated to make life and political success a bit easier for him. Unlike his Liberal predecessor in office, Alexander Mackenzie, Laurier came to power at a time when Canada was enjoying the effects of a buoyant world economy. The excess population of Europe and the end of the supply of free land in the United States brought hordes of immigrants to western Canada. The industrialized cities of Europe were ravenous for Canadian foodstuffs and the development of hardy new strains of wheat made it possible for Canada to supply that demand. British and American investment capital poured into the country.

The change in Canada through 15 years of Liberal rule was stupendous. Population and industrial production grew at a phenomenal rate. Winnipeg, the gateway to the West and a town of 26,000 in 1891, boasted a population of 136,000 in 1911. Calgary grew from 3,800 to 44,000 people in those same years. Agents from Clifford Sifton's department scoured the British Isles, the United States and continental Europe luring immigrants to "the last best West." In 1896, 20,000 immigrants arrived; in 1903, over 100,000; in 1906, 190,000 and in 1913, 402,000. Between 1896 and 1911, over 1,000,000 people of all nationalities settled on the prairies.

Eastern Canada was expanding too. Montreal, the country's largest city grew from 328,000 residents in 1901 to 491,000 in 1911, while Toronto's 1901 population of 210,000 almost doubled in the same period. These new urban immigrants, while facing a dozen new and different hardships, could find work in the industries springing up everywhere. The country's output of manufactured goods increased in value from $215 million in 1900 to $564 million in 1910. Laurier seemed positively prophetic when he stated that just as the nineteenth century had belonged to the United States, "the twentieth would belong to Canada."

With the enormous influx of immigrants into Canadian cities during the early 1900s, slums like this one in Montreal began to spring up.

Laurier and the Liberal party claimed credit for this remarkable growth even though international developments were more directly responsible. But the Canadian electorate was not about to quibble. They were enjoying the prosperity and in the elections of 1904 and 1908, they responded positively to the Liberal request to "Let Laurier Finish His Work." In the first election, the Liberals won a majority of 63 and in the second, a majority of 50.

With this mandate from the voters, Laurier moved boldly on the domestic front. Though his economic and political measures were certainly not original, they were rewarding. Basically, Laurier was successfully extending John A. Macdonald's National Policy. Macdonald spoke about immigrants; Laurier and Sifton brought them. Macdonald implemented a system of tariffs; Laurier and Fielding preserved and refined them. Macdonald stressed the importance of a transcontinental railway and built the CPR; Laurier agreed and built even more rail lines.

Immigration was the key to Canada's development. Immigrants would make the railways profitable; they would produce the wheat a hungry world desired; and they would provide a huge consumer market for everything which Canadian industry could produce. The

A Prosperous Nation

tremendous flow of immigrants into Canada and especially into the West was primarily the work of Clifford Sifton. Coming from Manitoba, Sifton was an incredibly energetic minister who was thoroughly committed to the rapid settlement and development of the West. His agents spread throughout Europe, established countless immigration offices in the British Isles and advertised extensively throughout the United States. Sifton offered inducements and simplified the procedure by which immigrants could claim homesteads.

Laurier's own influence on immigration policy was subtle and indirect. French-English relations, not immigration per se, were his primary concern. His work was to impress upon his ministers and upon the country the need for ethnic tolerance. There was, he stressed, no single Canadian identity. Instead there were two identities, one French and one English, and both had to be respected. Assimilation was impossible and indeed undesirable. He rejected the notion, which many English Canadians endorsed, that Canada had to have only one language, one culture and one religion

Agents from the Canadian immigration department gave lectures throughout England to encourage people to settle in "the land of opportunity."

in order to be a nation. He urged his ministers and all Canadians to be tolerant of diversity.

Laurier's attempt to promote an acceptance of diversity was fundamentally successful. His primary concern had been the French Canadians, but the principle was extended to include immigrants. The government would exercise little overt pressure upon them to assimilate quickly. They would not be compelled to discard their own culture and adopt the language, religion, values and standards of the majority. With time, assimilation might occur, but it would come gradually and without animosity.

Laurier's values were partially responsible for the development of the Canadian mosaic. Mennonites were permitted to establish their own German-language schools. Mormons, forced out of the United States by its assimilationist laws, found a refuge in the Canadian West. Ukrainians, with their strong sense of national identity,

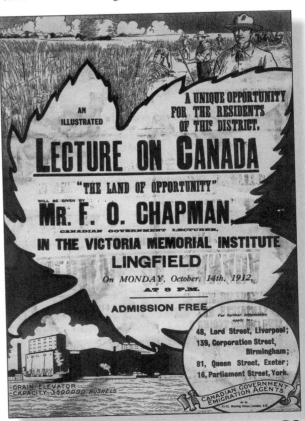

were allowed to establish their own distinct churches and to preserve their language in isolated prairie communities. Jews could adhere to their culture. Russians, Poles, refugees from the Austro-Hungarian empire, even Doukhobors and Hutterites, the "refuse of the world" as one critic called them, were all permitted to live and develop largely as they wished. Canada had its problems, of course. Immigrants from Asia and African-American immigrants from the U.S. faced hostility wherever they settled. But Laurier's government never accepted blatant discrimination or intensive assimilationist policies.

This generous attitude was difficult for Laurier to maintain. Political pressures mounted urging him to adopt a more restrictive immigration policy. Many English Canadians, convinced of their own superiority, wanted Canada to admit only Anglo-Saxons, Germans and Scandinavians. Many French Canadians were similarly opposed to an open-door immigration policy though for different reasons. They were jealous of the attention paid to immigrants and the aid given to their settlement efforts. They feared that the French-Canadian proportion of the population and their political

Massive waves of immigration during Laurier's tenure lead to a truly multi-cultural Canada.

"NOW THEN, ALL TOGETHER"!

A Prosperous Nation

importance would decline with this massive influx. Laurier, of course, tried to appease his critics. In 1905, he named Frank Oliver from Edmonton as his new minister responsible for immigration. Oliver, unlike Sifton, was not terribly sympathetic toward those "stalwart peasants" in their sheepskin coats. However, even with Oliver in office, the flow of immigrants continued unabated. These new Canadians were simply too important to exclude; the country's economic growth depended upon them.

Another factor crucial to Canada's development and Laurier's political success was the railway. As immigrants poured into Canada, as wheat production in the West soared and as business expanded everywhere, the Canadian Pacific Railway was unable to meet all the demands placed upon it. It had been built in the 1880s to serve the needs of the 1890s; but twentieth-century Canada had exceeded even the dreams of those who developed the first National Policy.

In 1902, Laurier began negotiating with C.M. Hays of the Grand Trunk Railway Company and William Mackenzie and Donald Mann and the Canadian Northern Railway. The Grand Trunk had its lines in central Canada while Canadian Northern ran many short lines in the West. The sensible approach would have been to combine the efforts of these two organizations and create a second transcontinental railway from the Pacific to Quebec City. But the two groups were rivals and refused to pool their resources in spite of Laurier's persuasive efforts. Laurier then changed tactics. Ignoring the objections of both Clifford Sifton and A.G. Blair, his minister of railways, Laurier pushed through measures which resulted in Canada having two competing transcontinentals, as well as the CPR, by World War I. Economically, this approach to the railways was indefensible and during the war both new lines had to be nationalized to save them from bankruptcy. They had been built more on optimism than on any accurate assessment of Canada's potential. A.G. Blair, not Laurier, understood railways, and he resigned from the government to protest the prime minister's interference and intransigence.

In spite of Blair's criticism, Laurier actually knew what he was doing. He was not a hard-headed businessman; he was a politician who responded, sometimes too quickly, to the emotional demands of the electorate. And these railways, like the CPR for Macdonald, were a political bonanza. His railway policies would win votes in the West where farmers needed better service and where the CPR was universally unpopular. His policies would be applauded in Ontario where industries would be busy supplying everything that railway construction required. His policies would attract the support of financiers in Toronto and Montreal since they would result in handsome dividends. Quebec too would be pleased, since it saw the new lines as an elaborate aid to northern colonization schemes. Laurier had been under pressure from Israel Tarte to do more for colonization in Quebec. In fact, Tarte had been forced to resign from the cabinet on that issue, and Laurier had to ensure that he did not carry French-Canadian votes with him. Finally, the Maritimes, which had always been neglected by federal governments, would appreciate the Winnipeg to Moncton section of the line and the jobs which its construction would bring.

Laurier's grandiose railway policies made political, though not economic, sense. As the Opposition, federal Conservatives would have to criticize Laurier in Parliament. Laurier could then present himself to the public as the only leader who truly appreciated Canada's potential. He could present his plans for a great Canada, as Macdonald had done, and denounce the Tories as prophets of gloom and doom. Early in the twentieth century, most Canadians endorsed the prime minister's vision.

Tariffs constituted the last portion of the National Policy which Laurier had to consider during his years in office. The tariff issue had been a costly one for the Liberals throughout the years. In 1878, Macdonald beat the Liberal party by promising a system of protective tariffs. In 1887 and again in 1891, the tariff question figured prominently in the Liberal defeats. The party itself had always been divided on the question. Men like Richard Cartwright condemned tariffs because they raised the cost of goods and lowered the standard of living for most Canadians. Others such as Blake and Fielding felt that some tariffs were necessary to stimulate and protect Canadian industry from foreign competition. Laurier himself never felt strongly one way or the other, but he did recognize the emotional and symbolic value of this issue. Tariffs symbolized the determination of Canadians to create a country economically and politically independent of the United States. Tariffs were the price Canadians had to pay to be Canadian.

In 1893, Laurier had convinced the party to abandon free trade as one of its policies. After 1896, he discreetly returned to the issue and extracted every ounce of political value from it. His treatment of the tariff question exemplifies his moderate, conciliatory and somewhat opportunistic style of politics. The 1897 budget delivered by Fielding dealt with the tariff question by offering something to everyone. For the majority of Canadians who believed in the tariff, Fielding offered only a few minor changes. Some tariffs were abolished (on binder twine for example); others were reduced somewhat; and others were slightly increased. But the overwhelming majority of tariffs was left untouched. For free traders, still strong in the party, and for imperialists, whose support the party needed, the Laurier government offered an "imperial preference." While the general tariff remained high, a somewhat lower rate was placed upon goods imported from great Britain. Free traders thought this was a step toward no tariffs; imperialists thought it a step toward imperial federation. The government appeased the vast majority and offended few.

Laurier, however, would go no further in either direction. Imperial federation was impossible, as was free trade, since both would have frustrated Canada's desire to become an economically independent, industrialized nation. Canadian manufacturers, always a strong force politically, were not willing to allow the duty-free entry of any product which could be manufactured in Canada. For 12 years after this first budget, the Laurier government merely tinkered with the tariff. It was refined, made more flexible and, according to the Liberals, made more equitable.

In 1910, Laurier and the Liberal government, searching for a dramatic new election platform, once again adopted the idea of free trade. This was very much in response to the plight of western farmers, a plight which Laurier learned of during his lengthy 1910 tour of that region. Farmers were hard hit by the tariff. Because of it, they had to pay more than American farmers did for everything they purchased. They paid more for tractors, for harvesters, for overalls, for shoes and so on. Yet when selling their grain on the international

An 1891 Conservative election campaign poster?

market, they had to compete with those very same American farmers. Since the efficiency of Canadian farmers was no greater, their profits were obviously lower.

In October 1910, Canada began trade negotiations with the American government and by January 1911 a settlement had been reached. The Canadian negotiators had pressed their American counterparts vigorously, since like all Canadians, they were confident of Canada's ability to go it

A Prosperous Nation

43

Laurier addressing a crowd in Edmonton, Alberta, during his extensive 1910 tour of the West

alone if need be. The subsequent reciprocity agreement was everything they had asked for and something which all Canadian prime ministers since 1866, including Macdonald himself, had hoped for.

The trade agreement could only stimulate the Canadian economy. Products of the farm, forest, mine and fishery were able to enter the vast American market either duty-free or at a very low rate. In return, a very limited number of manufactured goods could enter Canada at a reduced rate. Canada retained the right to end the agreement at any time as well as the right to extend its terms to British imports. Everyone, Laurier thought, should be happy with the agreement: imperialists, free traders, westerners, farmers, fishermen. Even manufacturers had no grounds for complaint. The Liberals and Laurier were delighted, and the Conservative Opposition in Parliament was downcast.

But Laurier was growing older now. He no longer controlled the country as he once had. His well-laid plans and bold initiatives backfired and the accumulated errors of long years in office soon caught up with him.

A Prosperous Nation

Chapter 6
An Accounting of Errors

Sir Wilfrid Laurier and other Canadian dignitaries waiting to receive the Prince of Wales in Quebec City during the 1908 Quebec tercentenary celebrations

By 1911, the mistakes and inadequacies of a decade and a half of governing finally took their toll on Laurier. Two characteristics had marked Laurier's many years in office. First, his primary goal had been to lessen French-English tensions in the country. Laurier had set his sights on this goal early in his career and if need be, all else would be sacrificed to it. Second, to accomplish this, Laurier himself had to remain in power. To stay in power, he had to remain in office. To stay in office, he had to maintain his political grip on Quebec while taking care not to completely alienate Ontario and the rest of English Canada.

By the end of his administration, Laurier, older now and less adept, had lost Ontario. But the loss of Quebec was even more decisive and disheartening. For many of the French Canadians and especially for nationalists like Bourassa, Laurier was just too anglicized. He was perceived as a *vendu*, one who had sold out to the English. He always spoke English in the House of Commons. He often seemed to regard the concerns of the nationalists as petty and parochial. He had been knighted and seemed to relish the attention lavished on him in England. Most galling though was the fact that he took Quebec for granted. Convinced that Quebec would mindlessly follow him because of his French background, Laurier appeared more concerned with courting Ontario's affections. Whenever French and English Canadians clashed over a particular issue, such as participation in the Boer War, it was the French Canadians who had to relent. Laurier's brand of compromise, according to the nationalists, was a one-way street: only the French Canadians, following Laurier's direction, were compelled to compromise. They alone, and not English Canadians, had to modify their vision of Canada for the sake of national unity.

French Canadians were deeply disturbed by the separate schools question which arose in the new provinces of Alberta and Saskatchewan in 1905. To French Canadians, this was the Manitoba schools question all over again and involved their rights as Canadian in all parts of Canada. In 1896, Quebec had elected Laurier expecting that its interest would be better protected by a French Canadian prime minister. Quebec was to be disappointed.

In 1905, following a great deal of pressure from the West, Laurier drafted and introduced an Autonomy Bill of the North West Territories. In an attempt to appease French Canadians and the Catholic hierarchy, still simmering over their loss in Manitoba, Laurier's bill provided for separate, denominational schools in the two new provinces of Alberta and Saskatchewan.

English Canadians were appalled. They generally opposed separate schools as a matter of principle. They also opposed these schools because their existence would seem to give the French-Catholic church too much influence in a religiously mixed society. More important though, English Canadians wondered about Laurier's self-professed belief in provincial autonomy, for here was an example of the federal government dictating educational policy to two provinces. Laurier obviously was no more a "provincial rights" advocate than the federal Conservatives had been in the 1890s when they tried to coerce Manitoba. Laurier, in spite of the principles behind his 1896 campaign, appeared willing to ride roughshod over the provinces for the sake of a few votes and a few blessings in Quebec. Here was a man who had spent his life fighting an aggressive church establishment only to give up and begin catering to it in 1905. It also seemed that Laurier was willing to bully his own party, since both western and Ontario Liberals were known to oppose separate schools. Even Clifford Sifton, the minister responsible for the West, had been ignored as Laurier confronted his party and Parliament with this new legislation.

An Accounting of Errors

A TERRIBLE ROW!

Sifton rushed back to Ottawa from his Florida vacation, resigned his post in the cabinet and then rallied both Conservative and Liberal opponents to the bill. Before long, with his prestige and authority weakened, Laurier relented and a new bill was introduced. The revised measure left the question of separate schools for the new provinces to decide. This was a striking defeat for the prime minister, since it was generally believed that Alberta and Saskatchewan would not tolerate denominational schools for long.

Laurier's actions cost him votes in English Canada and support in Quebec, where Bourassa and other French-Canadian nationalists portrayed him as the betrayer of Catholic interests. A mass meeting in Montreal during April denounced Laurier for not fighting Sifton and for backing down on the schools question. Catholic and French-Canadian rights were supposed to be sacred and not subject to the prime minister's personal whims or political needs. The Canadiens had begun to reject Laurier.

The rejection was intensified five years later when Laurier introduced his Naval Bill. This measure was a compromise between the militaristic demands of the imperialists and the isolationist attitudes of the Quebec nationalists. The act created a small

This cartoon by J.W. Bengough depicts one of the incessant arguments between English and French Canadians about how "British" Laurier had become.

An Accounting of Errors

47

Sir Wilfrid Laurier,
Landsdowne Park, Ottawa

Canadian navy and paid lip-service to the ideal of imperial unity. Yet, like the Autonomy Bill of 1905, it satisfied no one. French Canadians screamed that Laurier was going too far while English Canadians screamed that he was not going far enough. Both sides were rejecting his middle-of-the-road policy. As Canada was growing more prosperous and self-confident, compromise solutions became unsatisfactory. Both French and English Canadians wanted bold new initiatives, something which the old government could no longer offer.

Laurier was growing older himself and his grasp of just what Canadians wanted was growing weaker. This was evident during the 1905 and 1910 debates, but it was even more evident in 1911 when he presented his proposed reciprocity treaty with the United States. When Laurier went to the polls on this issue, he had been superbly confident. The treaty would bring the Liberals success and the country increased prosperity. Negotiations with the Americans had gone well, and the treaty was favourable to Canada; surely nobody would deny that.

However, many English Canadians rejected Laurier's assumptions, and it became clear that the interests of Laurier and the Liberal party no longer reflected the interests of everyday Canadians. The Conservative party, ably led by Robert Borden and efficiently organized by the former Liberal, Clifford Sifton, successfully exploited Canada's strong anti-Americanism. Canadians, they explained, had fought in 1775 and in 1812 for a distinct country; Canadians, led by John A. Macdonald, had devised a National Policy and a tariff system to ensure and to perpetuate Canadian independence. Now, they claimed, all might be lost. The Laurier Liberals, with their continentalist approach, were threatening the very existence of Canada.

Canada's industrial, financial and banking interests, fearing what reciprocity might bring, turned against Laurier. Workers, fearing for their jobs, turned against Laurier. Even many farmers, miners and lumbermen, fearing American competition and the precariousness of the agreement, turned against Laurier. The election of 1911 was a complete reversal of the 1908 results. The three Maritime provinces gave a slight majority of their seats to the Liberal party, but that was where Laurier's fortunes ended. Westerners, for whom reciprocity was primarily designed, elected 18 Conservatives and 17 Liberals;

An Accounting of Errors

Ontario, the heartland of industrial and imperial Canada, elected 73 Conservatives and only 13 Liberals. Meanwhile Quebec, upon which Laurier had always relied, gave only 38 of its 65 seats to his party. An unholy and short-lived alliance of Bourassa nationalists and Borden Conservatives had thrown Laurier out of office.

Reciprocity, a Canadian navy, imperialism, separate schools — these were all important issues, but they alone do not account for the defeat of Laurier's party. Concrete issues often have less impact upon the electorate than one would expect. In his younger days, Laurier understood this and had relied upon his style and personality to sway voters. In 1896, in 1900 and in 1904, Laurier and his party were zealous, progressive, energetic and charismatic. By 1911, after 15 exhausting years in office, Laurier and the Liberals were none of these.

In 1896, Laurier, new to power, rather insecure and certainly respectful of the talents of others, had constructed a superb cabinet of dedicated, forceful and effective men. He had acknowledged their abilities and rarely interfered in their departments. However, the years of office and the honours that accompanied it had fed Laurier's ego. He now had confidence only in himself. The country depended on him; national unity depended on him; the government and the party depended on him. He knew best and the job of his ministers was to implement his directives.

In 1902, Laurier had dismissed Israel Tarte for endorsing a program somewhat different from his own. This was the same Israel Tarte who had been primarily responsible for the 1896 Liberal victory in Quebec. Old allies now lasted only so long as they served the prime minister's purposes. A.G. Blair left the cabinet in 1903 when Laurier, ignoring Blair's plans for expanding Canada's railway grid, forced his own policy on the cabinet, the party and the House of Commons. And Clifford Sifton left the cabinet in 1905 over the Saskatchewan-Alberta school question.

By 1911, only one of the strong ministers elected in 1896 remained — W.S. Fielding. But he, like Laurier, was older now and less effective in the cabinet and with the voters. Age had slowed them both down. Too be sure, much of the party was growing older. The young William Lyon Mackenzie King, for instance, noted in his diary that many ministers dozed off during cabinet meetings. Sir Allen Aylesworth, the minister of justice and one of the old war-horses, was almost deaf and unable to hear most of the proceedings. Yet Aylesworth led the Liberal party in Ontario (it was no wonder that the party fared so poorly there).

Laurier was often urged to replace some of these exhausted men. But he invariably rejected such suggestions and continued to appoint

Israel Tarte

aged associates because they "never made any trouble for me." At this stage in his very long career, Laurier did not want to rock the boat. He was still enough of a realist to appreciate that his days as prime minister were numbered, and he wanted his remaining days in office to go unruffled.

The new men he did bring into the cabinet were generally ineffective. They owed their personal success and their office to Laurier. They admired him, usually offered unquestioning obedience and generally failed to keep the prime minister and the party in touch with modern issues. M.P.'s known to have a strong will, known to be zealous reformers and known to force issues were denied cabinet rank by Laurier.

In 1909, Laurier created a separate Department of Labour and made Mackenzie King its first minister. Ever since his university days in Toronto and Chicago, King had been concerned with the increasing number of poor people in Canada's urban centres. In the remaining years of Liberal rule, King did introduce some positive legislation and made a name for himself, but his endeavours were minimal compared to the extensive problems of the working class. He was held in check because Laurier, a man shaped by the nineteenth century, was less interested in industrial workers than in farmers. Laurier appreciated that King was an able man, but Laurier's preoccupation was with French-English relations in Canada and not with labour, a modern issue.

By 1911, Laurier was out of touch with Canada. Voicing their disapproval, Canadians voted down the Liberal administration and elected a new, energetic one led by Robert Borden. A new political cycle was beginning and after 15 years of wielding power, Laurier was once again the leader of the Opposition.

The desertion of Quebec had been especially hard on Laurier. The nationalists, he believed, had been duped and misguided. They could not live in harmony with the Conservatives for very long, and once the split came — as it did in 1912 and 1913 over Borden's own naval policy — where would Quebec be? The Québécois had been responsible for Laurier's defeat and Laurier, whatever his faults, still believed he was their best guarantee for protection within Confederation. Laurier, not Bourassa, was the only French Canadian with a large, nationwide following. Laurier, with his compromising ways, had at least toned down the bitter French-English hostilities that had always divided Canada. Rejection by Quebec was a harsh blow politically and an unkind cut personally for Wilfrid Laurier.

Chapter 7
Last Efforts

Laurier was not complacent about his defeat. Although it was not totally unexpected, it still was humiliating for a proud 70-year-old man after 40 years of public life. As Sir Wilfrid, he had grown accustomed to robust cheers not the bitter jeers which greeted him in Montreal. He had spent so many years trying to reconcile French and English Canadians; now he wondered whether his life's work had all been in vain. He still believed that Ontario had rejected his party so overwhelmingly because he was a French Canadian. "It was not reciprocity that was turned down," he claimed, "but a Catholic premier."

He was bitter about Quebec. Certainly he had not given Quebec everything it wanted; but no man could, especially since its wants were defined by Henri Bourassa. Bourassa was an impractical idealist, almost a demagogue, who harmed Quebec by polarizing hatreds in Canada. Laurier had compromised — that was true enough — but what else could he do considering the fact that English Canadians constituted the majority? Laurier was also bitter about Armand Lavergne, the son of Emilie and one of Bourassa's most dogmatic and vehement disciples. Had he no loyalty? Had Bourassa, Quebec and even Canada no sense of loyalty? Had they all no respect for him? Jubilant Conservative partisans had even tried to parade in front of his house, but Robert Borden vetoed their plans.

Laurier spent the next two weeks putting on a show of calm for the press and trying to wind up old business. Laurier, the masterful politician, tried to take care of his friends, promising new constituencies to the many loyal ministers who had been beaten — Fielding, Mackenzie King, Sydney Fisher, George Graham and so on. But he no longer had power to wield or patronage to dispense. Party unity and partly loyalty were, for the first time in 15 years, difficult to enforce.

Laurier sought a bit of peace during the entire summer of 1912 in Arthabaskaville. He was happy sitting in the shade of the maple trees, surrounded by friends and neighbourhood children whom he entertained with stories from Canada's past. Sometimes he was a bit long-winded, but his listeners were usually respectful of this digni-fied older gentleman. Emilie Lavergne was no longer a supporter —

their relationship had cooled because of her son's political activities and because Laurier had not appointed her husband chief justice of Quebec. But now Zoe provided the companionship Laurier needed. They had been married for almost 50 years and Zoe, like Wilfrid Laurier himself, had matured. She was Lady Laurier now and filled the title with grace and charm. She had become politically active and astute, had chaired several committees and now even enjoyed life in Ottawa.

Laurier pondered the possibility of retirement and was tempted to remain in Arthabaskaville. After all these years, he certainly deserved the rest and tranquillity. But Laurier was not the lazy young man of the 1870s and 1880s. With its organization in shambles and its ranks decimated, the Liberal party still needed

Lady Laurier and Sir Wilfrid

him; and as its leader, he still had battles to fight. He remained sufficiently egotistical to believe that the Canadian voters had made a mistake in 1911. He remained sufficiently aggressive to want to turn the tables on the Conservative-nationalist alliance. At this stage in his career, however, he was most concerned with completing his life's work, the reconciliation of French and English Canadians.

Quite consciously, Laurier became more the elder statesman than the active politician. He was appalled by the strident nationalism evident in Quebec and was distressed by the anti-French sentiments in English Canada. He dedicated himself to recapturing Quebec from Bourassa, even if that meant losing votes in Ontario. Canada, he felt, needed his approach, even if the Liberal party did not. Between 1912 and 1918, and for the first time since the 1880s, Laurier became somewhat estranged from the party rank and file and on several occasions had to fight party rebels who wished to adopt a more popular policy.

His desire to win back Quebec from Bourassa was a liability elsewhere in Canada, but Laurier was now willing to sacrifice power. Much more than office was at stake. The continued existence of Quebec within Canada was involved as was Laurier's own place in Canadian and French-Canadian history. Laurier wanted to be remembered as the unquestioned and most prestigious leader of his own people. For that, he would sacrifice all possibility of regaining office.

Before long Laurier was given an opportunity to redeem himself in French-Canadian eyes. In November 1912, Parliament convened and Robert Borden introduced his own Naval Bill. Fearing the growing German menace and wishing to reward Ontario for its support, the Conservatives proposed that Canada contribute $35 million directly to Britain for the construction of three huge dreadnoughts, the mightiest ships ever built. Borden's proposed contribution, reeking of colonialism and imperialism, ruined Bourassa as a political force in Quebec since he had endorsed the Conservatives in 1911. Many French Canadians now regretted that they had deserted Laurier and by 1914, many politicians were again predicting a Liberal sweep of Quebec in the next election. If Laurier won 60 of Quebec's 65 seats, he could regain power even though Ontario opposed him. With this prospect in mind the Liberals filibustered in the House of Commons and finally killed the Naval Bill in the Liberal-dominated Senate. But Borden, having access to the same political intelligence as Laurier, chose not to call an election on the issue.

A second issue also helped Laurier recoup his strength in Quebec. In 1912, the Ontario government, responding to strong assimilationist pressures, introduced Regulation 17 which severely restricted the right of Franco-Ontarian children to French-language schools. Quebec was outraged as were the parents of the children affected. The debate was fierce and French-English rivalries were intensified.

Laurier, as a French Canadian and as the leader of the Liberal party, was in a horrendous dilemma. By defending the minority, he would not only be interfering with provincial jurisdiction but he would also divide his party and weaken it in Ontario. On the other hand, he was still devoted to the ideals of mutual tolerance and minority rights. Tolerance, not assimilation, was the way to unite the country. Besides, neither Borden nor the provincial Liberals were defending the minority.

Laurier placed party considerations aside and in May 1916 supported Ernest Lapointe's introduction of a motion urging both sides to be generous and asking for the restoration of the minority's language privileges. In his own speech, Laurier appealed to all the members' sense of justice and tolerance. As he had anticipated, the Liberal party divided on the issue with the western and Ontario members initially opposing the resolution. However, when Laurier wrote out his letter of resignation over the issue, most of the party returned to the fold. Though his power was fading, Laurier still had sufficient political strength to defend his principles.

The most difficult issue of this period emerged out of World War I. There was no question in anyone's mind about Canada's participation; when England was at war, its colonies were automatically at war. When the conflict began in 1914, all Canadians, both French and English, were enthusiastic, perceiving it as a just and necessary war. But as the war dragged on into 1916 and 1917, as more and more Canadians died in the trenches of Europe and as the country exhausted its human and natural resources, serious doubts arose.

On the one side were most English Canadians, including Borden and his government. They continued to see the war as one between right and wrong. It was not simply Great Britain's war, but the Christian world's war and Canada's war. Anything that contributed to the Allies' victory had to be done regardless of the cost. By January 1917, this commitment obliged the government to introduce the Military Service Act, providing for the compulsory conscription of 100,000 men between the ages of 20 and 45. Though it might be unpopular, conscription was necessary because, according to one minister, "The war is paramount

World War I Canadian recruitment poster

and transcends everything else."

The French Canadians meanwhile, after their initial enthusiasm had waned, did not believe that the war should transcend "everything else." With time, the French Canadians began to perceive it as just another European power struggle, the result of the aggressive imperialism Bourassa had been condemning for almost two decades. It was Britain's war, not Canada's war. Why should Canadians die and why should domestic Canadian development cease for the sake of Great Britain? Why should French Canadians fight to defend "freedom" when Ontario was denying "freedom" and French schools to its French minority? Why should French Canadians fight in any army which clearly discriminated against them and which was led by a notorious Orangeman, Sir Sam Hughes?

Henri Bourassa and French Canadians in general did not want Canada to pull out of the war; they simply wanted Canada to put its own needs first and limit its involvement. And they did not want to be compelled to fight. If English Canadians wanted to enlist, let them. If French Canadians wanted to, let them. But it was morally wrong and absolutely indefensible to introduce conscription and force people into uniform.

Once again, Sir Wilfrid Laurier found himself in the terrible predicament of having to find some middle ground. He appreciated that both French and English Canadians felt very strongly about the war and conscription, and he appreciated that neither would accept a compromise. Complicating the situation were his own feelings on the matter and his compelling desire to bring Quebec back under his influence. But the Liberal party would not be content to kill itself politically just to curry favour in Quebec.

Though some Liberals felt Laurier was willing to ignore the party for Quebec's sake, Laurier certainly never saw his actions in that light. He felt his moderate approach was right, even if it was not politically expedient. Laurier never wavered in his support of the war effort, delivering countless speeches in Quebec urging all French Canadians to contribute. (He worked so hard that in September 1915, he suffered a physical collapse.) Laurier combined his patriotic appeal with a political one during the early stages of the war. Repeatedly, he chastised the government for mismanagement, for tolerating profiteers, for its part in the Ross rifle scandal. He also condemned Borden and Hughes for needlessly alienating Quebec.

Laurier's political strategy seemed to be succeeding until French-Canadian enlistments fell off drastically and the Borden government decided to form a "union government" to introduce conscription. Laurier was aghast. On principle he recoiled from the

"Over the Top;" Canadian troops in the trenches of World War I

use of coercion for anything. He had spent a lifetime fighting it; he could not change now.

Borden invited Laurier and a number of his colleagues into the union government. Though some of his followers wanted him to accept for political reasons — refusal would be suicide in English Canada — Laurier firmly rejected the offer. Borden was not seeking Laurier's opinion on conscription, for the government was determined to implement it, with or without Laurier, and only wanted his name and prestige. If he joined, it would mean renouncing his principles and deserting Quebec.

Laurier's outright refusal caused considerable rumblings in Liberal party ranks, but Laurier still hoped to salvage his political career. He tried offering a compromise; instead of simply imposing conscription, he said, let there be a referendum on the question. That would remove the coercive element. In this way he hoped to appease both French and English Canadians. But Laurier's proposal was impractical. In a referendum, Quebec would have voted "yes." Then what? Laurier would still have to opt for one or the other.

Last Efforts

A recruiting office in Acton, Ontario

Laurier's compromise was also impractical because few Liberals would accept it. Many of his old colleagues, old friends and old supporters were deserting him now. They were bypassing their leader, joining the union government and endorsing conscription. Laurier saw them as traitors to the party and as political opportunists, but he was wrong. Fielding, John W. Dafoe, the influential editor of the *Manitoba Free Press*, and the others were, like Laurier himself, principled Canadian nationalists, but nationalists who had a different concept of the country's duty during this difficult period. Canada had a great responsibility and could not avoid it simply because Quebec, in their minds, was terribly parochial. Laurier, as Liberal leader, had set the party on a particular course and since he could not be persuaded to relent, they had no choice but to leave the party and join Borden.

Thus, with only a small remnant of the once powerful Liberal party behind him, the 76-year-old Wilfrid Laurier fought the general election of December 1917. It was a gruelling campaign made all the more difficult by Borden's Wartime Elections Act. This legislation gave the vote to soldiers and to female relatives of soldiers while disfranchising many immigrants. Soldiers, their wives, mothers and daughters were almost certain to vote for the government, while the immigrants, thankful for Laurier's generous immigration policy, were

This cartoon appeared in the *Manitoba Free Press on Dec. 15, 1917. John W. Dafoe, who had recently shifted his support from the Liberal party to the Union Government, was the editor of this newspaper.*

most likely to vote Liberal. Laurier waged an energetic campaign in spite of his age and his now fragile health. He spoke in Winnipeg on December 10, Regina on the next day, and Calgary the next. He spoke at five meetings in Vancouver on December 14. Laurier was fighting desperately for his vision of Canada.

But Laurier did not stand a chance with the English-language press describing him as "the Kaiser's choice." Only Laurier's dedication and firm belief in the justice of his cause kept him going. The election results could have crushed Laurier, for they showed just how deep the divisions were within Canada. Eighty-two Liberals were elected of which 62 were from Quebec. Ontario returned only eight Liberals and the West only two. Laurier had succeeded in regaining Quebec's respect and support, but in what else had he succeeded? Almost 50 years before, he had entered public life in order

Last Efforts

to unite French and English Canadians. That had been his goal in life and politics. Judging from the nature and results of the 1917 campaign, he had failed. In 1837, shortly before Laurier's birth, the English in Canada had used military force to crush a French-Canadian uprising; in 1918, following the implementation of conscription, English-Canadian troops were again used to quell French-Canadian dissent.

Chapter 8
The Laurier Legacy

The election of 1917 and the disheartening 1918 conscription riots in Quebec marked the end of Laurier's political career and the virtual end of his life. He was 77 now, tired and often ill. In spite of this, he still held his position in the Liberal party and devoted time to it. His first task was to rebuild the party in order to regain power at the next election. The Liberal party, he believed, was the key to Canadian unity and Canadian prosperity. With the war's end, Laurier began this rebuilding process by welcoming back Fielding, Dafoe and the others who had left him.

In spite of his recent defeat, in spite of the venom poured on him by English Canada, Laurier remained serene and at peace with himself. He was satisfied with his life, with Zoe, with the respect Quebec again had for him, with the manner in which history would treat him. The sickly boy from humble origins in St. Lin had done well indeed. His long life had provided him with the opportunity to contribute greatly to the welfare of his province and of his country. He wished his final months could have been spent in the prime minister's office, but he had already enjoyed his share of honour and power.

Wilfrid Laurier

William Lyon Mackenzie King and his political father, Sir Wilfrid Laurier

As wartime passions cooled and Laurier himself reached the end of his days, he began to receive once again the accolades of English Canada. He was recognized as a great Canadian, a national builder much like John A. Macdonald. According to one of his fiercest opponents, Arthur Meighen, Laurier was "one of the finest men I have ever known."

Sir Wilfrid Laurier's greatest legacy to Canada was his insistence upon respect for the principles of British liberalism. He believed in the basic goodness of ordinary people and felt that their individual freedom and liberty had to be respected. He believed in protecting the weak and minorities against the strong and powerful. Thus in the 1870s he had defended French Canadians from ultramontanism; in the 1880s he had condemned the government for treating Louis Riel and the Métis unfairly; in the 1890s he had tried, in his own compromising way, to gain concessions for the Manitoba Catholics just as he later did for Francophones in Ontario. It was this same belief in freedom and liberty that, in 1917, had irrevocably blocked his efforts to regain office. He had sacrificed even power, which he loved, to defend those who opposed being compelled to join the army.

Laurier's respect for individuals and their different views and his principled rejection of coercion made him a great compromiser. Opponents, in Laurier's mind, might be wrong, but still their views had to be respected. Canada could and would be united only if everyone were as generous and tolerant as Laurier himself.

On February 18, 1919, Laurier died. There had been no lengthy illness and no great remorse. It was a dignified, serene death, in keeping with the man himself. He had lived a long and productive life. He had established standards which the Liberal party would continue to respect and had reconstructed the party in his own image. William Lyon Mackenzie King, a member of Laurier's cabinet and Laurier's successor as Liberal leader, served as prime minister for a total of 20 years. His success was due to his own remarkable abilities as a compromiser and due to his own appreciation of Quebec's sensibilities. King, like Laurier, avoided confrontation and viewed national unity as his primary goal. With more success than Laurier, King too fought conscription in World War II. King's successor as Liberal leader and prime minister, Louis St. Laurent, like Laurier, was a French Canadian and an elegant, graceful man. Laurier had made it possible for French Canadians to share in the government of their own country.

Great men must die of course, but their example, their spirit, their ideals live on. Laurier was a great man. He had his faults — he could be haughty, egotistical and too insistent that the Liberals respect his personal wishes. But no person is without fault, and Laurier's only strengthen his humanity. Though far from perfect, he was a living person, warm and friendly, at times passionate and at times serene. He could mix with people and win their devotion, just as his long and distinguished career won him the undying devotion of the country he loved. He was a great Canadian who did all he could to ensure his country's unity, harmony and prosperity. He did as much as any person could.

The Laurier Legacy

Further Reading

Berger, Carl. *Imperialism and Nationalism, 1884-1914.* Toronto: Copp Clark, 1969.

Brown, R.C. and R. Cook. Canada, *1896-1921: A Nation Transformed.* Toronto: McClelland and Stewart, 1976.

Cartwright, Richard J. *Reminiscences.* Toronto: William Briggs, 1912.

Dafoe, John W. Laurier: *A Study in Canadian Politics.* Toronto: Thomas Allen, 1922.

David, L.-O. *Laurier, sa vie, ses oeuvres.* Beauceville: L'Eclaireur Limitée, 1919.

Granatstein, J.L. *William Lyon Mackenzie King.* Don Mills, Ont.: Fitzhenry & Whiteside, 1976.

Hall, D.J. *Clifford Sifton.* Don Mill, Ont.:Fitzhenry & Whiteside, 1976.

Langelier, Charles. *0. politiques de 1878 à 1900.* Quebec: Dussault et Proulx, 1909.

Neatby, H.B. *Laurier and a Liberal Quebec.* Toronto: McClelland and Stewart, 1973.

Robertson, Barbara. *Sir Wilfrid Laurier: The Great Conciliator.* Kingston: Quarry P, 1990.

Rumilly, R. *Sir Wilfrid Laurier.* Paris: Ernest Flammarion, 1931.

Schull, J. Laurier: *The First Canadian.* Toronto: Macmillan, 1965.

Skelton, O.D. *Life and Letters of Sir Wilfrid Laurier.* Toronto: Oxford University Press, 1921.

Wade, Mason. *The French Canadians, 1760-1967.* Toronto: Macmillan, 1968.

Credits

The publisher wishes to express its gratitude to the following who have given permission to use copyrighted illustrations in this book:

Canadian War Museum, page 36

Metropolitan Toronto Library Board, pages 12, 19, 31, 62

Public Archives of Canada, page 3 (C9082), 7 (PA27537), 9 (PA26528), 16 (C15876), 20 (C20052), 21 (C51786), 23 (C3833), 27 (C17964), 28 (C1860), 30 (C8427), 38 (C80430), 39 (C63440), 48, (PA51531), 53 (PA26986), 55 (C29484), 57 (PA648), 59 (C9040), 61 (C1973), 63 (C5851)

Public Archives of Manitoba, page 14

Public Archives of Ontario, pages 10, 32, 34, 44, 45, 48, 58 (A.T. Brown Collection)

Every effort has been made to locate copyright holders. The publisher will welcome any information that will allow it to correct any errors or omissions.

Index